GREAT YARMOUTH
Volume 2

A Second Portrait in Old Picture Postcards

by

Len Vincent

To Liam
Best Wishes
Len Vincent
Xmas 1992

S. B. Publications

Dedicated to my daughter Alison and my son Timothy

First published in 1992 by S. B. Publications
c/o 19 Grove Road, Seaford, East Sussex. BN25 1TP

ISBN 1 85770 034 1

Typeset and printed by Geo. R. Reeve Ltd., Wymondham, Norfolk NR18 0BD.

CONTENTS

CONTENTS

CONTENTS

Front Cover: Old Toll House, Library and Museum, c. 1930.

INTRODUCTION

During my research for this second volume illustrating Great Yarmouth and district in old picture postcards, I was reminded constantly of the hard life that many people endured in the 'good old days': the poverty, the dangers that many workers faced during their long working days, and the lack of medical care that we take for granted. The seven-day prison sentence a wanderer received for being found sleeping in the shelter near the revolving tower, the young girl who was scalped whilst scrubbing the factory floor, having caught her hair in a revolving belt, and the father of twelve children pleading with the guardians of the town to be allowed to work for three days (the waterways were built by the unemployed), and the stigma of residing in the workhouse (later to be called the infirmary to raise its image, and now converted to the Northgate Hospital). A man residing at the workhouse when applying for a job, and having work ability, was advised to change his address and re-apply. I have a great admiration for those people, who endured so much.

I have to thank too the many photographers of the day who set up their tripods and cameras and left the legacy that enabled me to recall those days. One such photographer was Alfred William Yallop, a Londoner, who came to seek the benefit of Yarmouth's bracing air for his health in 1889 and decided to make it his home. For over a quarter of a century he had a shop at the top of Regent Road (see p. 56). A. W. Yallop became Mayor of the Borough in 1925, and in recognition of his services to the town an avenue bears his name.

Another photographer to whom I am grateful is Donald R. Nobbs, a Diss man by birth, who learned his craft in Blackpool and Hull and came to Great Yarmouth in 1920 taking over the studio of Mr. W. Banger in Regent Road. In 1929, having realised that newspapers were using more photographs, he became a press photographer and London picture editors would wire him for photographs for a news story.

Donald Nobbs was appointed official photographer to the shore naval base established at Great Yarmouth, H.M.S. *Miranda, Midge* and *Watchful*. Most of his work was confidential and secret, because during the war, photographs were subject to censor.

Among his unusual assignments during his career was the job of progress photographer whilst the Haven Bridge was built in the 1930s. It meant crawling through and setting up his cameras in the four-feet diameter tunnel that runs below the River Yare. I would like to take this opportunity of thanking his son for allowing me to reproduce some of his work.

There is an old expression 'every picture tells a story' and I trust that the reader will find truth in this well-known phrase, and many memories in these pages.

THE FISHERMEN'S HOSPITAL, p.u. 1907

The Fishermen's Hospital was built in 1702 at a cost of £621 for 'decayed fishermen'. It comprised of twenty cottages each having two rooms. Only infirm fishermen and their wives were accepted as the occupiers of the cottages; applications being received from persons over 60 years of age. Within the quadrangle are two statues: one in the cobbled courtyard depicting Charity; and the other depicting St. Peter which stands above the courtyard housed in a cupola. A restoration scheme in 1961 resulted in the twenty original houses being converted to ten. Note the milk hand-cart, and the apex of the building behind which was the Methodist Temple. This has been demolished to make way for the relief road known as Temple Road.

1

ROYAL PROCLAMATION, 1910

The Mayor of Great Yarmouth, T.W. Swindell, stands on the site of the old Market Cross declaring the death of King Edward VII. The original market cross stood on the site from 1385, was replaced in 1509, and the last one erected in 1604 until its demolition in 1836 by the Reformed Town Council. Notice the crowd of onlookers on the balcony of Fishstall House (now Millett's and Boots). The shops to the left of the public house were all fish merchants, and in the left background the shop on the corner of Fish Street was occupied by a hairdresser.

HEDGES LTD., MARKET PLACE, c. 1908

The corner of Market Place and King Street was occupied by Hedges Ltd., bootmaker. Photographed by A. W. Yallop, the postcard shows an amazing display of boots and shoes, some advertised at 12/- (60p) per pair. The house was formerly used by Mr. S. S. F. Stafford, a surgeon. On the left hand side of King Street, the shops were occupied by: Miss Wright, tobacconist; Smith and Daniels; domestic bazaar; and Boning Bros. store (the larger sun blind).

POSTMEN ON PARADE, 1911

The postmen of Great Yarmouth on parade on Mayor's Sunday, on their way to St. Nicholas Church. In the right background stands the Market Place post office, now the Halifax Building Society. Notice the different ladies' hats and the postmen's caps.

SMITH'S STORE, p.u. 1911

A fine display of clearly priced hardware at Smith's Stores which was situated at 12–13, South Market Road. In 1916 they moved to premises at 8, South Market Road and traded there until the early 1940s. During its lifetime the shop at 12–13, South Market Road has served as a drapers, fishmongers and a Co-op. In 1935 it was converted to a private house with the fascia and plinths of the store still remaining today.

The Toll House Museum, Middlegate Street, Great Yarmouth. No. 1170

TOLL HOUSE, 1920s

Little is known of the origins of the Toll House. In 1362 it was owned by Stephen de Stalham, but how it became vested to the corporation is unknown. It was the seat of civil government for the borough of Great Yarmouth for many years. The dungeons were used for prisoners for 600 years, the last prisoner being discharged in 1879.

ROW 20, c. 1920

Known in later years as Two-Necked Swan Row, Row 20's earliest recorded name was Wrestlers Tap Row named after a tavern that existed here. The row runs from the Market Place to Howard Street North formerly known as Charlotte Street. The workshop of Frank Forder, cabinet maker was situated at 13, Row 20. After extensive damage was caused, following a bombing raid in 1943, the area was rebuilt and part of the original course of the row can still be seen today.

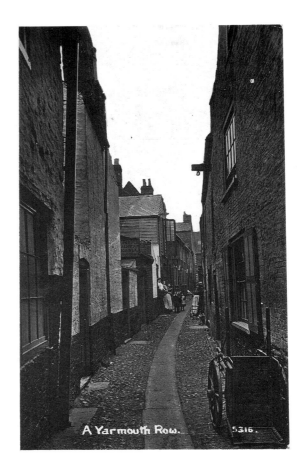

A Yarmouth Row.

GARIBALDI GENTS IN BLOATERLAND

Sherman, Photo., Gt. Yarmouth.

J. POWELL, PROPRIETOR.

GARIBALDI HOTEL, c. 1910

Joe Powell became the licensee at the old Garibaldi Tavern, a small public house, in 1890. By 1899, following many extensions and improvements, the Garibaldi had been converted into a four storey hotel with accommodation for 500. The hotel was run as a 'Gentlemen Only' establishment; the boarders known as Yarmouth United Lambs until the first world war, and then known as the Gari Boys. They were renowned for their charity work in supporting the local hospital but were still frowned upon for upsetting the more genteel class of holidaymaker. However, their fame spread and the Gari continued its success. Joe died in 1926 but the hotel carried on his tradition until the outbreak of the second world war.

GARFIELD HOUSE, c. 1912

Garfield House was built in 1886 with its original address as 14—15, Caister Road; now renumbered and situated at 46, Northgate Street. The premises were first occupied as a builder's yard but became G. E. Shalder's garage in the early 1900s. The business was subsequently taken over in the early 1920s by George Cooper who carried on trading until 1969, when his son took over the business until 1989. It was one of the first garages in town to sell petrol; this picture taken before the pumps were installed. Note the number plate of the car in the doorway, F 172.

BEACONSFIELD ROAD, p.u. 1912

Photographed from North Denes Road and showing the Earl of Beaconsfield public house and the chimney of the corporation refuse destructor in the background. The end house of the first row of terraced houses was converted into a shop by a Mr. William Lambert. Today, the railway lines and signal on the left have been removed and the area is now a car park. Where the line of saplings are, there now stands a row of magnificent trees.

10

PETERBOROUGH BOARD RESIDENCE, CAISTER ROAD, NEWTOWN, GT. YARMOUTH

PETERBOROUGH HOUSE, c. 1930

Peterborough House, adjacent to the Corporation nurseries, was one of the few properties that stood on the west side of Caister Road (known as Caister Causeway in pre-war years). After it received severe bomb damage during the war, the house was vacated, and subsequently demolished to make way for new housing in 1954. The buildings in the right background were holiday chalets.

WALPOLE ROAD, c. 1920

A rare view of Walpole Road, built in 1887, looking north towards Balmoral Avenue. Today, most of the houses are holiday establishments and numerous cars are parked either side of the road. Notice the sign for 'Capstan' cigarettes on the wall of the corner shop.

Fowlers Central Camping Ground, Caister Road, Gt. Yarmouth.

FOWLER'S CENTRAL CAMPING GROUND, c. 1935

Fowler's Central Camping Ground was situated adjacent to Peterborough House and between the River Bure and Caister Road. Mr. Fowler can be seen entering his shop in the right foreground. The camp site was sold to Messrs. Steward and Patteson in 1939 and the Bure Hotel was built in its place. In the background can be seen Smith's potato crisp factory with two of their lorries, probably bearing that famous logo 'if you wish to pass please sound your horn'.

In the late 1980s both the factory and the Bure Hotel were demolished for housing development.

BARNARD AVENUE, p.u. 1924

Of the many trees pictured in this view of Barnard Avenue only five remain today. The air of peace and tranquility has now disappeared, as this road is now a very busy route from the sea-front to Caister Road.

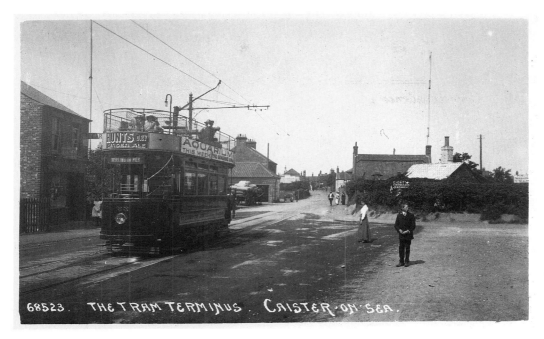

THE TRAM TERMINUS, CAISTER-ON-SEA, 1912

To cater for the needs of holidaymakers and Caister residents, four new trams were purchased and a tram route opened on 16th May, 1907. The first tram, driven by the Mayor, Mr. F. Arnold, departed at 12.30 p.m. and arrived in under ten minutes at the Green Gate public house. The public service began at 2 p.m. and ran every twenty minutes for a fare of 2d. per person. The postcard can be dated accurately because the advertisement for 'The Sunshine Girl', a musical revue staged at the Royal Aquarium, was playing in August 1912. Geo Allen, motor-cycle engineer, moved his shop to the building to the left of the tram in 1911, and today this is part of Allen's car showroom and garage.

HIGH STREET, CAISTER-ON-SEA, c. 1930

Jesse Jones' shop, known as The Old Post Office, was established in 1846. The mail was delivered by cart from Yarmouth at 8.00 a.m. and collected at 6.00 p.m., weekdays only. In 1883 John Thomas Blyth, a shoemaker, became postmaster and rebuilt the shop. A plaque bearing a Victorian crown and the initials J.T.B. can be seen today over the doors. In 1912 the post office moved to new premises in Yarmouth Road. Postmen were based and letters sorted at Caister until 1965 when the work was transferred to Yarmouth. Notice the attractive gable end of the King's Arms, right background, since rebuilt and moved further back.

WATER TOWER, 1932

On the 13th May, 1853, an act was passed to supply Great Yarmouth and district with water from the Great Yarmouth Waterworks. The first open reservoir was situated near Caister Church and the adjacent covered reservoir containing $1\frac{1}{4}$ million gallons was built in 1896. With the continuing growth of the town, the insufficient pressure of water was becoming a problem and it was recommended a water tower be built. On 22nd October, 1932, the new concrete-steel water tower constructed by Trussed Steel Concrete Co. of London was formally inaugurated by the Lord Lieutenant of the county, Mr. Russel Colman. The tower is 161ft. 9ins. in height, has a capacity of 784,000 gallons, and the internal diameter of the water tank is 75ft 6ins. The tower is built of 4,000 tons of material, including 175 tons of reinforced steel and 512 tons of cement. The tank is electrically connected to Ormesby Pumping Station and water is taken from Ormesby Broad and the River Bure.

BOATMEN'S SHED, CAISTER-ON-SEA, c. 1907

This boatmen's shed stood in the vicinity of Beach Road. The bell on the left was used to summon help to launch and beach their boat. These 'old salts' could possibly be two of the forty members of the Company of Beachmen in Caister. The Beachmen's official purpose was 'the saving of property, rendering assistance to vessels or ships aground, stranded or wrecked on the sands or beach'. The Company was disbanded in 1941. Today, the shed no longer exists; another victim of the eroding coastline.

KING'S ARMS, CAISTER-ON-SEA, c. 1911

A bowling green was advertised as an attraction for the King's Arms public house before its modernisation. A carrier stands outside the old post office and the wireless station mast can be seen in the distance.

THE CASTLE GALLEON ON HEMSBY BEACH

THE *CASTLE GALLEON* ON HEMSBY BEACH, 1932

The 400-ton steamship had anchored near the Cockle lightship, opposite Winterton during a fierce and bitter gale when both her anchor cables snapped. At 4 o'clock on 28th February, 1932, the Newcastle collier was driven by an East North East wind, force 6 to 8, over one of the dangerous shelves of sand that abound along this coast and she became stranded on Hemsby beach. Flares from the lightship brought the Winterton Lifesaving Company to the scene and, under the supervision of Lieut. James Maquire, M.B.E., District Officer of Coastguards, eleven of the crew were rescued by Breeches Buoy. One of the crew, 'Hardcase Taffy' had been shipwrecked four times. The captain, Mr. J. Robson, and mate refused to leave the ship. It was some five weeks before the vessel was refloated on 2nd April, 1932.

4831 THE STORES, POTTER HEIGHAM.

POTTER HEIGHAM, p.u. 1908

Mr. Watts' Stores sold groceries, provisions, haberdashery, boots and shoes, and postcards. Today the store serves as the village post office.

4834 STATION ROAD, POTTER HEIGHAM,

POTTER HEIGHAM, p.u. 1908

A group of cyclists pause at a quiet corner of the village. The railway crossing gates in the background have since given way to a bypass. The hut advertising Cadbury's cocoa belonged to Mr. Watts' stores (see page 21). The brick wall on the left has gone and the premises that lie behind are now occupied by a restaurant.

THE GREEN, MARTHAM.

THE GREEN, MARTHAM, 1905

Martham, a large parish and attractive village, has a delightful mix of Georgian houses and cottages surrounding The Green in the centre of the village. Martham derives its name from the pine-martens which abounded in the area. In the right foreground, the grocery delivery boy stands outside the house which is a fish and chip shop today. The building on the extreme left is Martham Baptist Church, which was built in 1874. As early as 1323, a parish priest taught grammar to twenty boys of the village and a Free School was built as long ago as 1622.

BLACK STREET, MARTHAM, c. 1905

Black Street looking south facing the village green. The houses on the right and Mudd Cottages have since been demolished but the houses in the distance remain and can be identified by their distinctive supports. The first doorway in the left foreground is number 22.

Somerton Road, Martham

SOMERTON ROAD, MARTHAM, p.u. 1905

The trees and hedgerows have long gone from this scene of Somerton Road looking west. Blackthorne Cottage with its delightful thatched roof in the foreground remains today. The tower of the church of St. Mary the Virgin, known as the 'Cathedral of the Fleggs', stands in the right background.

MARTHAM STATION, p.u. 1905

Situated on the Rollesby Road not far from the village centre, Martham Station was opened by the Great Yarmouth and Stalham Light Railway Co. in 1878, later to be incorporated with the M. & G. N. in 1893. During the summer months it ran seven return journeys daily plus a late night service to Great Yarmouth, which continued until the summer season of 1958 when the line was closed. The building with its ornate bargeboard still stands today and was used commercially until recently.

WHITE STREET, MARTHAM, c. 1905

Why has the photographer captured this group of children? Could the occasion have been a Sunday School outing or a school outing? Maybe the bearded gentleman at the back was the schoolmaster? In 1905 the population of Martham was 1,211. In 1990 the population stood at 3,019.

HARLEY ROAD, c. 1925

Little has changed in this view apart from a further storey added to the house on the corner of Salisbury Road.

CHURCHILL ROAD, GREAT YARMOUTH.

CHURCHILL ROAD, p.u. 1907

One or two of the locals turned out to watch the photographer who had moved some fifty yards into Churchill Road
before taking this photograph, looking north. The junction with Salisbury Road can be seen close to the shop blind on the
left.

BEACH STATION (M.G.N.R.)

A superb photograph of a D 0-6-0 tender engine standing in Yarmouth Beach yard. The station opened on 7th August, 1877 and was part of the Great Yarmouth and Stalham Light Railway. The isolation of the station caused the arrival of its first locomotive to come via Vauxhall, which then had to be taken along the street tramways as far as the Town Hall where temporary track had been laid through the town; the journey taking two days to complete! The original line ran from Nelson Road North to Ormesby. It reached Hemsby and Martham by 1878 and Stalham two years later. The rear of numbers 44—49, Wellesley Road can be seen in the background.

BEACH STATION STAFF, Summer 1925

Station Master A. P. Coe and Police Constable Brown are amongst this staff photograph taken outside Beach Station. The station closed on 28th February, 1959, with the last train leaving at 10.25 a.m. and returning at 11.14 p.m. It is believed that some of the staff pictured here served on that train. Two iron stanchions bearing the logo of M.G.N. and E.M.R. together with a small section of track still remain in the coach and lorry park that occupies part of the former railway.

ROYAL VISIT, 1931

The first royal visit to the borough was in 1382 when Edward II came to view the fortification of the town. The most frequent royal visitor was the Prince of Wales, who visited the town no less than eight times. This postcard shows the Duke and Duchess of York attending the N.U.T. conference held on the Britannia Pier on the 9th April, 1931.

THE PARK CHAPEL, p.u. 1909

The Park Baptist Church was built on St. George's Denes in 1863 by Mr Emmerson, a building contractor, and constructed of Suffolk brick with white stone facings at a cost of £1500. The memorial stone together with a bottle containing coins, a copy of *The Freeman* newspaper and a bill announcing the service was laid by J.J. Coleman of Norwich on 26th August, 1863. The local Baptist Church originated with the Norfolk & Norwich Baptist Home Missionary which held its first service in November 1860 in the Corn Hall, Regent Street with seventeen members present. At the time of writing the church is in the process of being rebuilt.

Goode's Hotel. Gt. Yarmouth. Central Position, Facing Sea. Restaurant à la carte.

108125 8 C. Turner, Gt. Yarmouth.

GOODES HOTEL, c. 1910

In the late 19th century, two brothers, John and William Goode, purchased Winton's Rooms, formerly the residence of Lord Berners. The Goode brothers established a dancing academy here and in 1901 alterations were made to convert it into a hotel. In September of the same year the premises caught fire, which destroyed Winton's Rooms. In June 1902 a new building known as Goodes Hotel and Ballroom came into being, which enjoyed many years of successful trading. Today, the hotel has closed and the ground floor is occupied by an amusement arcade.

SAND ARTIST, c. 1930

One of the attractions on Yarmouth beach was the artistry of the sand sculptor, Mr. F. Bultitude, who was born in 1911 and at the age of three was stricken with infantile paralysis. Among his many creations were *Rock of Ages,* Sir Malcolm Campbell's *Bluebird,* Christie the murderer, Lord Nelson, and a scene from the film *Duel in the Sun.* He would change his work every two or three weeks, according to the popularity of the subject. The only tools he used were a wooden knife and a duster. At the beginning of the season he would sink a barrel into the sand and pay children to fill it with sea water, enabling him to dampen his work. To avoid his efforts being vandalised, he often had to patrol his site until 2 or 3 in the morning. Mr. Bultitude retired in 1960.

HOLKHAM HOTEL, p.u. 1906

The Holkham Hotel was also known as The Glass Barrel and this postcard shows the hogshead-size coloured-glass barrel suspended by a block and tackle above the doorway. Another storey to the building at the rear has been added since the photograph was taken. The forecourt, where the jockey scales stands, is now the site of a modern bar. What happened to the Holkham Hotel's distinctive glass barrel?

THE COLUMBIA.   H. J. ELLIS, Proprietor.   *Sherman, Photo., Great Yarmouth.*

THE COLUMBIA, p.u. 1906

The Columbia is situated on the corner of Crown and Apsley Roads. It still retains its original name today but is also known as Toni's Taverna. The ivy-covered house has also become part of the restaurant and the doorways have been altered since this photograph was taken. EX 6, possibly the first motor brake to operate in Great Yarmouth with Mr. W. Bartram at the wheel, gave trips along the sea-front at a cost of sixpence (2½p).

MARINE PARADE, c. 1905

The Eastern District Coastguard Station on the sea front had a frontage of 152 feet and a depth of 170 feet. The buildings were grouped around a central courtyard: the south side used as offices and also housing the station officer's house; one of the two houses on the north side housed the District Officer. At the rear were eight cottages. The horse drinking trough was removed at the time of the demolition of the station (see Vol. 1, page 35) and is still in use at the cab rank adjacent to the Britannia Pier.

SHIPWRECKED CREW, 1912

Between 5 and 6 o'clock on Monday morning, 26th August, 1912, the booming guns from St. Nicholas lightship roused many people to watch the launch of the Gorleston Lifeboat towed by the tug *Yare* in what was described as hurricane conditions. The lifeboat proceeded in the direction of Scroby Sands where they found the steamer *Egyptian* stranded on the cross ridge. She was bound for Newcastle from Antwerp with a cargo of cement and iron, with a crew of thirty-three including the captain's wife and child. The lifeboat *Mark Lane* made four trips to bring her crew ashore. Many salvage attempts were made, but by Wednesday afternoon she was abandoned as a wreck. This picture was taken at the rear of the Shipwrecked Sailors' Home and shows some of the crew of the *Egyptian*.

YARMOUTH LIFEBOAT, c. 1908

No shortage of willing hands to pull the *John Burch* number ON 3299 from its station situated on the sea front. The *John Burch,* donated by Mrs Burch in memory of her husband was built by the Yarmouth firm of Beechings in 1892 at a cost of £240 and remained in service until 1912. The lifeboat station built in 1859 for £375, closed in 1919 and during its lifetime saw 151 launches and helped save some 302 lives.

WELLINGTON PIER AND MARINE PARADE, c. 1903

A brake carrying holidaymakers passes the junction with St. Peter's Road, a main thoroughfare to the sea front and second only to Regent Road in the early 1900s. At the jetty entrance can be seen one of two cannons, veterans of the Battle of Sebastapol. These were a great favourite with children but were removed in 1939. Notice the tramlines, the jockey scales and the lady selling her wares from linen-lined baskets.

The Jetty.

YARMOUTH.

No. 832. Jarrolds' Series.

Printed in Germany.

THE JETTY, p.u. 1903

A jetty has existed in Great Yarmouth since 1560; Admirals Duncan and Nelson among the many famous people to have landed here. Yarmouth's sea front was noted for its many windmills and look-outs. Prior to the days of the lifeboat, beachmen companies were formed to undertake rescue and salvage work connected with the shipping off the coast. These look-outs, usually built of heavy timber and well braced to withstand gales and heavy tides, were manned night and day by one or more hardy beachmen with telescopes. In 1835 the cost of a look-out was recorded as £62.11.4d. and the tallest one was to the west of the Barking Smack public house. The look-out in this picture stands in the centre left background.

42

GROCERY STORES,
ST. GEORGE'S ROAD, c. 1909

Samuel Berry stands outside his general grocery stores with a well-stocked window showing familiar names such as Camp coffee, Huntley & Palmer's biscuits, Chef sauce and Chiver's fruits. In the 1920s the shop became the Brooke Bond Wholesale Tea Warehouse, but since the war the shop has been converted to a hairdresser's salon.

43

FIRST CLASS
LANDAUS
BROUGHAMS
DOG CARTS
WAGONNETTES

FOR HIRE

TELEPHONE 0233
NORFOLK HOTEL STABLES
ST. GEORGE'S ROAD
GT. YARMOUTH

WILLIAM WORTON, JOB MASTER, c. 1910

William Worton pictured outside his premises at 45, York Road (the window can still be recognised today). The Norfolk Hotel was a few yards away on the sea front. By the 1930s, Worton & Sons were advertising a motor-car hire service, and a garage still exists fronting St. George's Road next to the Norfolk & Norwich public house. Landaus are still a feature of Yarmouth's sea front today.

ST. PETER'S ROAD, c. 1922

A bill poster with his barrow can be seen at work in the left foreground, and a coal merchant with horse and cart stand outside the Wellington Hotel. Although most of the buildings have changed their use today, the post office situated bottom right still remains.

ST. PETER'S PARSONAGE, p.u. 1910

The foundation stone of St. Peter's Church was laid in July 1831 and the church was consecrated by the Bishop of Winchester on 16th August, 1833. St. Peter's was the town's acting parish church after St. Nicholas was blitzed in June 1942 and remained so until the rededication of St. Nicholas caused its closure in May 1961. In 1967 it was rededicated for use by the town's Greek community and became known as St. Spyridon's Church. The postcard shows the parsonage situated on Dene Side which is now occupied by a hotel. Most of the trees have been removed and the ground has been built upon to allow car parking and an extension to the hotel.

SCOTS FISHERFOLK, c. 1934

During the fishing season, a familiar scene on Yarmouth's streets was the fish merchants' lorries, with their wooden seats, which called at lodging houses to collect the workers. This photograph was taken outside the Church of Scotland Rest Rooms and the First Aid Station situated on St. Peter's Road; the latter now the home of the British Red Cross. Although James Sutherland no longer has a base in Great Yarmouth, they are still trading in Scotland. Note the children's fashionable headgear.

Bombed and Machine Gunned M.V. "RECULVER,"
Tuesday, January 9th, 1940.

Photograph shows the Havoc wrought on the bridge and
machine gun bullets in the funnel, caused by enemy aircraft
in the North Sea.

Copyright Photograph by
D. R. NOBBS, Great Yarmouth.

(This photograph has been passed by the Ministry of
Information).

M.V. *RECULVER*, 1940

M.V. *Reculver* was one of Trinity House's service vessels to lightships. During a routine trip to exchange lightship crews after Christmas leave in 1940, it was attacked by a Dornier bomber. The *Reculver* had offered no provocation and was completely defenceless. The savage attack on the ship resulted in the death of Second officer George Purvis, thirty injured men and very extensive damage.

THE NELSON COLUMN

The column was designed by William Wilkins of Norwich who also designed the Shirehall at Norwich. The first stone was laid in 1817 and the column was completed in 1819, fourteen years after the Battle of Trafalgar. The people of Norfolk contributed £7,000 towards its building costs — a fortune at the time. The monument, also known as the Norfolk Pillar (its correct title) is 144 feet high and has 217 steps to the top. The figure of Britannia at the top has her back to the sea looking towards Nelson's birthplace at Burnham Thorpe. Nelson visited Great Yarmouth three times and was given the freedom of the borough in 1800. In 1981 Britannia and the six figures of victory that support her, were found to be in poor condition and were replaced by glass-reinforced plastic replicas.

10 GREAT YARMOUTH — The Nelson Column. — LL.

49

THE MISSIONS TO SEAMEN INSTITUTE, 63, South Quay, Gt. Yarmouth. *Yallop, Photo.*

THE MISSIONS TO SEAMEN INSTITUTE

The Missions to Seamen Institute was started in 1858 in Row 139. In 1900, premises were built at 63, South Quay (now renumbered No. 40); this picture showing the austere 'recreational' room. It received serious bomb damage during the last war, but was rebuilt after 1945. The premises were sold in 1969 when the Mission moved to Angel House, Southtown Road. The port the premises were eventually sold in 1983.

SOUTH TOWER, p.u. 1910

In 1262 Henry III granted the inhabitants of Great Yarmouth a charter to enclose the town with a wall and fosse to protect themselves from invasion. The cost of building, local jealousies and the 'Black Death' plague were amongst the many reasons it took 111 years to complete. When it was completed, the town had fortifications consisting of an almost semi-circular wall, 2,280 yards long, 23 feet high and seven-feet thick, with ten gates and twenty towers. Still standing today, with a public right-of-way cut through, is the Blackfriars Tower. The group in the foreground are probably connected with Adam and Eve Gardens (demolished in post-war development).

V332-20   YARMOUTH. SOUTH TOWER.   RAPID PHOTO. E.C.

51

NET REPAIRING, GREAT YARMOUTH.

NET CHAMBERS

A unit of netting was known as a lint, a linca thread derived from flax. In the 19th century, lints were made of white cotton which had to be oiled by immersion in a mixture of linseed oil and a type of varnish, which were then passed through rollers to remove the excess. This process stiffened the net and they were edged with a fine cord known as twine masking after which they were ready to be tanned; a process which gave extra length of life to the cotton. The nets were then hung from the balconies of the net chambers or laid out on the South Denes to dry. A net was 8 feet deep and 8 feet long when laid flat.

A TYPICAL GREAT YARMOUTH ROW, c. 1930

There are many postcards of Yarmouth's Rows; the most famous being Kitty Witches Row whose history has been recorded many times. This card is one of the author's favourites, as the photographer has not only captured the sunlight and shadow but also the irregular structure of the timber, the brickwork, the stones and the many chimney pots that created the unique character of the Yarmouth Rows.

TYPICAL GT. YARMOUTH ROW. J 6907.

KING STREET, GT. YARMOUTH.

KING STREET, p.u. 1907

King Street in the snow and photographed before the Victoria Arcade was built in 1926. In the centre is Starling's, hatters; and to the right, the old established jewellery business belonging to Aldred and Son which has now ceased trading.

Tom Green's Corner, Gt. Yarmouth.

TOM GREEN'S CORNER, p.u. 1909

Shops certainly used their windows to full capacity in the early 1900s and no doubt their sunblinds to protect their fine array of wares. Tom Green occupied this shop on the corner of Regent Road and King Street until September 1988 when Greenwood's acquired the business. A sign above the shop points to the beach and a wall advertises the postcards of A. W. Yallop, the photographer whose work is featured on many of the postcards in Volumes 1 and 2. This postcard was used by Tom Green to order 3 dozen pairs of gents' fancy top knicker hose, lightweight, size $9\frac{1}{2}$ in July 1909.

Series by the Scottish Photographic Touring and Pictorial Post Card Coy., Glasgow.

This is the old shop. The size is the same, but the front is now more modern & smarter

FREDERICK MARSH, KING STREET

Frederick Marsh established his jewellery and fancy goods business in 1836 and traded in King Street (see Volume 1, page 57). In the early 1900s, he advertised watches from 3/6d. each. He also traded as a pawnbroker and amongst the unredeemed pledges for sale were sewing machines, bicycles, a pair of massive bronze horsemen and beautiful china tea services. What tales of hardship lay behind these items?

KING STREET, c. 1917

A tramcar used as a mock-up tank passes along King Street as part of the war effort to sell War Savings Certificates. The building on the right was Divers public house, erected in 1856, which claimed to be the first business premises to install electric lighting before the town supplied a power supply in 1894.

REGENT ROAD, GREAT YARMOUTH, c. 1960

The white building facing the camera was occupied by J. Lyons restaurant during the pre-war years. During and after the war it became Boots the Chemist. The Regal Theatre, later became the ABC and then the Cannon, was built on the site of the old Yarmouth Theatre and opened on 1st January, 1934 showing a film entitled *The Private Life of Henry VIII* starring Charles Laughton and Merle Oberon. It was built by local builder, J. Balls & Son of Northgate Street, and was demolished in July 1989. The tudor-style building on the right was built by B. G. Beech of Dene Side and opened on 13th July, 1929 by Councillor H.T. Greenacre who congratulated the Directors of the Electric Company for enhancing the centre of Yarmouth. It stood on the site of Town Wall House and provided showrooms, offices and a workshop for the town's Electric Company. Sadly, the building was demolished to make way for the town's shopping precinct.

76 REGENT ROAD, p.u. 1907

Until the 1980s, this building has always been connected with catering. Notice the fine glass chandeliers hanging in the window, with hocks of ham and sauces displayed in the left-hand window. The door to the left leads to Henry Thomas Greenacre's restaurant. The building is now occupied by a fashion shop.

76, REGENT ROAD, GT. YARMOUTH.

59

PRIMITIVE METHODIST CENTENARY,
1807—1907.
GREAT YARMOUTH CELEBRATION DAY,
SUNDAY, 21ST JULY, 1907.
[YALLOP

PRIMITIVE METHODIST CENTENARY, 1907

Methodism began in Great Yarmouth with preachers coming from Norwich and holding open-air meetings on Hall Quay, with a wagon serving as a pulpit. Known as The Ranters, five men were taken into custody for causing an obstruction on Hall Quay in 1854. Indoor meetings were held in a hayloft on Hog Hill (Priory Plain) and the Methodist Temple was built near to the spot in 1875. To mark the centenary, a day of celebration was held on 21st July, 1907 with meetings as early as 7.00 a.m. and continuing into late evening. At 2 o'clock, Methodists gathered in the Market Place and marched to the New Recreation Ground via Northgate Street and Kitchener Road, arriving at the Sandown Road entrance. The postcard shows Mr. Swindell announcing the opening hymn of the service, the music being provided by a harmonium.

SOUTH GATES ROAD Yarmouth

The recent floods caused trouble like this all over the Town. G.

21/1/05
[Photo by F. H. Sayers.

1905 FLOODS

Women and children lean out of the windows of one of Lacon's beerhouses, with even the horse turning its head for the photographer, in this view taken in South Gates Road. The extent of the damage to the town can be seen by comparison to the postcard in Volume 1, page 75. A flagpole can be seen jutting out from a store, a feature prominent on many pre-war buildings.

THE FERRY HOTEL, 41 SOUTH QUAY

Situated on the corner of Row 129 and South Quay, the Ferry Hotel was formerly known as the Newcastle Tavern. Previously this house and an adjoining property were a fine mansion where the Johnson family lived. In 1671 Sir James Johnson entertained Charles II in the house, receiving his knighthood for his hospitality. In 1867 there were no fewer than 18 public houses on South Quay.

Gipping Herrings, Gt. Yarmouth

BEECHING'S YARD, c. 1909

Scots fisher girls photographed in Beeching's boat yard in Southgates Road. In their early days, the Beechings were noted for their fine beach yawls. Later they concentrated on building herring drifters and by the time the business finished in 1926 they had built 137 drifters. In 1851 James Beeching won the national competition for the best designed self-righting lifeboat. The houses on the left are situated across the river in Boundary Road.

FLOODED AREA OF GREAT YARMOUTH

Bridge Road, Southtown

High Mill Road

Broken Bathing Pool wall

JANUARY & FEBRUARY 1953

Blackfriars Road

Boreham Road

Copyright: D.R.Nobbs

1953 FLOODS

On Saturday, 31st January, 1953, the worst floods in living memory hit the east coast. At Great Yarmouth the situation was worsened by the bursting of the banks of Breydon Water. It was estimated that 3,500 houses were flooded by 259 million gallons of water, and nine people lost their lives. This multi-view postcard depicts areas of Southtown and Cobholm, with the bottom left-hand picture showing the residents of 56, Blackfriars Road being rescued. The bottom right-hand picture shows Boreham Road which ran parallel to Blackfriars Road, and Louise Road can be seen in between 55 and 56, Blackfriars Road in the bottom left-hand picture.

VISIT OF HMS *YARMOUTH*, 1912

The fifth vessel bearing the name *Yarmouth* made a courtesy visit to the town in April 1912. Anchoring about a mile off the beach near the Britannia Pier, she was a second class cruiser of 5,250 tons built by the London & Glasgow Shipbuilding Co. of Glasgow. A celebration luncheon was held at the Town Hall after which a presentation was made of a silver replica Monteith Bowl 14" diameter and weighing 96oz. The other bowls shown were donated by the Countess of Leicester and the Port & Haven Commissioners. The ship was sold off in 1929 and the present 2,800-ton HMS *Yarmouth* was built in 1959.

GT. YARMOUTH AND THE RIVER YARE FROM THE AIR.

AERIAL VIEW OF GREAT YARMOUTH, c. 1929

The new Haven Bridge was being built at the time this aerial photograph of the town was taken. It illustrates vividly the density of the Rows, and the trees in St. George's Park. St. Nicholas, Market, Regent, Albion, Crown and Trafalgar Roads can be seen winding their way to the sea front. How many landmarks can you spot that are no longer with us? The white-faced stone of Arnold's and the curved frontage of the Conservative Club are two of many.

CROWN & ANCHOR HOTEL, c. 1910

Between Rows 59 and 61 stood two hotels on Hall Quay, the Crown & Anchor and the Steam Packet. Plans for rebuilding the site were submitted in February 1939 and the licence of the Crown & Anchor was transferred to Fowlers Camp (see page 13). The site was redeveloped and subsequently, in December 1939, part of the premises opened and became known as The Yare Hotel and traded as such until its closure in 1974. In 1978 it became the home of the Midland Bank. What a lovely splash of colour the hanging baskets and window boxes must have made to Hall Quay.

CROWN AND ANCHOR HOTEL, GT. YARMOUTH.

Char-a-Bancs, Great Yarmouth.

CHAR-A-BANCS, 1936—37

No trip to the seaside was complete without a journey to The King's Head at Belton, The Queen's Head at Burgh Castle, The Eel's Foot at Ormesby or The Village Maid at Lound. The four-in-hand brake held 32 passengers and the journey would cost 2 shillings (10 pence) or one shilling and sixpence (7½p) if trade was poor. A conductor would point out places of interest along the way and sometimes allow his imagination to create tales to amuse the visitors. There were also smaller brakes which carried 16 people drawn by two horses, or an exclusive landau could be hired by 5—6 persons for 10 shillings (50 pence). On the homeward journey the brake would sometimes be met by the sound of the post horn gallop. After the 1940 war a brake was sold to Collins of Blackpool to transport customers to his amusement park.

HALL QUAY, p.u. 1906

This view shows the development of Hall Quay (see Volume 1, page 70) after the telephone exchange had been built. Beezor's Old Furniture and China store was acquired by the Post Ofice in 1912,allowing the corner of Regent Street and Hall Quay to become the General Post Office at the hub of the town's commercial centre in the developing 1920s and 30s. The Post Office first occupied premises in Regent Street in 1871 and it was not until January 1977 that it moved its Head Office to North Quay; the corner of Hall Quay remaining a branch office. The first Post Office opened in 1695 in Row 107.

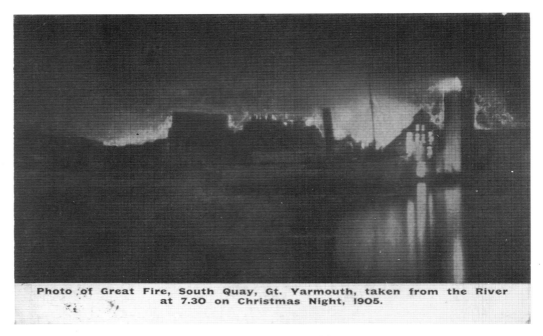

Photo of Great Fire, South Quay, Gt. Yarmouth, taken from the River at 7.30 on Christmas Night, 1905.

GRANARY FIRE, 1905

On Christmas night, a serious fire started at R. & W. Paul's granary on Southgates Road. At ten to six the alarm was raised and the custodian of the Corporation stables on Estcourt Road alerted to have horses ready to take the steam fire engine to the scene of the fire. It took 3 hours to bring the blaze under control. Within yards of the blazing buildings was F. Wenn's box-making factory and stacks of timber were in danger of spreading the fire, but heroic efforts by firemen and willing locals saved the situation. This photograph, taken from the western side of the river, shows the roof of the lofty elevator (built that year) alight.

TWO BEARS HOTEL, c. 1905

This photograph was taken before the rebuilding of the hotel in 1910 when a large part of the hotel was removed to widen the approach to Cobholm. There was a Bear Inn at the foot of the bridge (now the site of the thatched icehouse). Years ago travelling wild beast shows and menageries were held at various sites in the town, one being on Mill Road, so it is possible that the hotel derived its name from these visiting fairs.

PRESS'S HIGH MILL, GREAT YARMOUTH.
HIGHEST WINDMILL IN ENGLAND.
REGISTERED AT STATIONERS' HALL.   NOW RECENTLY DEMOLISHED.

PRESS HIGH MILL, c. 1900

Claimed to be the tallest windmill in England, Press High Mill had eleven floors and was built in 1812 at a cost of £10,000 for a Mr. Thomas Woolsey. For 92 years it dominated Yarmouth's skyline until it was demolished in 1904 after being auctioned for £100. The mill stood 120ft high, the diameter at its base was 45ft and the giant sails had a span of 84ft. A large open roadway ran through the base allowing the millers' carts and farm waggons to load and unload inside the mill. The mill worked day and night and was capable of grinding a ton of wheat or crushing 30 cwts. of oats every hour, justifying its huge cost. After its demolition some of its bricks were used to build a terrace of houses on Gatacre Road and the red chimney pots of nos. 35 and 36, Gatacre Road are said to mark the spot where this unique landmark of Yarmouth once stood.

COBHOLM WAR MEMORIAL, c. 1917

The scene at the dedication of the war memorial on 17th May, 1917. During the unveiling by the Mayor, Alderman E. W. Worlledge, M.A., five or six aeroplanes circled overhead. The memorial stood at the south west corner of the playground of the Girls and Infants' School, where four roads meet, designed by Arthur S. Hewitt and constructed by B. G. Beech of Deneside; the names of 750 men from the Cobholm district recorded on the eight panels of the octagon. It was during alterations to the school in the 1960s to become an annexe for the College of Further Education that the shrine 'disappeared'.

THE LOWER FERRY, p.u. 1907

A horse ferry near the present lower ferry was once the only means of crossing from Gorleston to Yarmouth. It was not until 1417 that the first Haven Bridge was built near a foot ferry; both ferries owned by the Lord of the Manor of Gorleston. One of the best known ferrymen was Mr. Robert Maystone Blyth who retired at the age of 66 after 45 years service and he estimated that he had rowed over 140,000 miles by making seven crossings an hour and working from 6 a.m. to 7 p.m.

THE CLIFF HOTEL, p.u. 1907

During the furious westerly gale which blew on Boxing Day 1915, the Cliff Hotel, one of the finest establishments of its kind on the east coast, was destroyed by fire. The fire started that evening on the third floor; the alarm raised by a passer-by who noticed a venetian blind ablaze. The fire brigade was assisted by the salvage tug *George Jewson* which had been brought up to the bend of the Brush Quay. The tug's pumps sent the water against the gale on to the top of the cliffs, but despite this great effort the hotel was completely gutted. The damage was estimated at between £50,000 and £60,000.

THE RUINS OF THE CLIFF HOTEL, 1915

Looking south-east and showing the devastation caused by the Boxing Day fire. Shortly after the fire, many thousands of people came to view the damage and the Gorleston tram cars reported that they had carried more passengers that day than they had done on any other day that year.

PIER PLAIN, c. 1910

Pier Plain showing the tram lines that ran from Southtown to Gorleston Beach. To the right of Mr. Gibbs' butcher's shop stood Middleton's the newsagent who for a number of years had many similar shops in the borough. Although the Hunts Dining Rooms sign has been removed the premises are still in use as a restaurant. Note the lone horserider.

MAYPOLE DAIRY CO. LTD., p.u. 1913

'Cool and firm' was the advertisement for this display of butter at the High Street branch of Maypole's. Before the days of refrigerated cabinets, keeping products fresh was a real problem and many a junior shop assistant had to rush the window display to the cellars during a sudden heatwave. Other branches of Maypole's were in Broad Row and King Street. The white-faced stone on the left of the postcard belonged to the Coliseum Cinema which opened in 1913 and stood on the site of Fishers Institute where magic lantern shows were given.

Family Gate

Gorleston Hospital

GORLESTON COTTAGE HOSPITAL, p.u. 1907

Nurses stand outside the ivy-covered Gorleston Cottage Hospital on Trafalgar Road. The hospital, opened in 1899 by Sir Henry Tyler M.P., contained 15 beds and one private ward. Children were accommodated in the general ward. The hospital closed in 1937 with the eight remaining patients being transferred to the new Cottage Hospital in Lowestoft Road by the Gorleston St. John Ambulance Brigade and police motor ambulance. Its use as a clinic continued until 1990.

VICTORY LOAN CAMPAIGN, 1918

Crowds gather on Feathers Plain to hear the Mayor, Alderman A. Harbord, launch the appeal for the Victory Loan Campaign. During the day two Anglo-Russian armoured cars toured the streets of Yarmouth and Gorleston in support (one can be seen in the left background). Peace celebrations were held over two days some ten days later, when 8,000 children and 4,000 ex-servicemen were given a meal. The men were entertained by concert parties or given tickets for a cinema show, and bonfires and fireworks brought the proceedings to an end. The two days celebrations cost the borough £2,800.

GORLESTON HIGH STREET

In March 1905, the Corporation took over the running of the tramways from the Yarmouth and Gorleston Tramway Co. Ltd. To celebrate the event, the Mayor, Alderman Mayo, drove a flag-bedecked No. 17 tram along Gorleston High Street.

BOYS BRIGADE ANNUAL CAMP, p.u. 1929

The Northampton Battalion of the Boys Brigade at their annual camp during August Bank Holiday week, sited on Gorleston Cliffs. 450 officers and boys travelled by train overnight and marched into the camp at 4.00 a.m. on the Saturday. The cost of setting up the camp on the first visit in 1912 was £20, but this had risen to £1,000 by 1929. Reveille was at 7.00 a.m. and lights out at 10.15 p.m. The Great Yarmouth Corporation horse-drawn water cart can be seen in the corner of the postcard, and a local tradesman's van is double parked.

Beach Gardens, Gorleston.

Buckland's Series No. 5.

We return to London in another twelve days. Will write you then our London address. My husband is not here.

BEACH GARDENS, p.u. 1903

The gardens and bandstand were erected in 1902, with military band concerts a feature of the holiday season in those early days. The Pavilion on the left was designed by J. W. Cockrill, Borough Surveyor, and opened in 1901. To the right of the Pavilion was the headquarters of The Rocket Lifesaving Co. now an amusement arcade. The Pier Hotel stands behind the bandstand. In July 1939, the Floral Hall (now known as the Ocean Room) and swimming pool opened on the site of Beach Gardens.

GORLESTON HARBOUR, early 1900s

A view of Gorleston Harbour, taken from Cliff Hill, before the shops were built on Riverside Road. The lighthouse built at a cost of £274 was designed to be seen two miles out to sea. The foundation stone of the lighthouse was laid by the Mayor, Mr. R. Martins, in April 1887. The pilot's house can be seen in the centre of the pier.

POST OFFICE, FRITTON, c. 1914

The hedges and ivy have long been removed from this rustic view of Fritton Post Office; a village once renowned for its decoy. Like so many small post offices it now opens twice a week, but when this postcard was issued it served its 227 inhabitants six days a week. The postmaster was Mr. W. Andrews, who was also a baker.

ST. OLAVES, c. 1930

Two lonely travellers appear on this view of Herringfleet Road. The white fencing marked the entrance to St. Olaves railway station. Today the woodland has been thinned and the road widened.

THE BELL INN, ST. OLAVES, p.u. 1910

The original Bell Inn, dating back to the late 13th century, served St. Olaves Priory, founded in the time of Henry III. It is known that an underground passage ran between the tavern and the priory, and that the Bell derived its name from its connection with the priory. Note the two large advertising signs on the wall of the inn. In the background, the gates of the level-crossing can just be seen.

ST. OLAVES STATION.

ST. OLAVES STATION, c. 1927

The station, part of the GER line that ran from Yarmouth Southtown to Beccles, was opened in 1859 and closed 2nd November, 1959. The sign next to the lamp post points to Fritton Lake, and housing now stands on the site.